Dad Gets Fit
and
Jobs on a Jet

Level 3 – Yellow

Helpful Hints for Reading at Home

The graphemes (written letters) and phonemes (units of sound) used throughout this series are aligned with letters and sounds. This offers a consistent approach to learning whether reading at home or in the classroom.

HERE IS A LIST OF PHONEMES FOR THIS PHASE OF LEARNING. AN EXAMPLE OF THE PRONUNCIATION CAN BE FOUND IN BRACKETS.

Phase 3			
j (jug)	v (van)	w (wet)	x (fox)
y (yellow)	z (zoo)	zz (buzz)	qu (quick)
ch (chip)	sh (shop)	th (thin/then)	ng (ring)
ai (rain)	ee (feet)	igh (night)	oa (boat)
oo (boot/look)	ar (farm)	or (for)	ur (hurt)
ow (cow)	oi (coin)	ear (dear)	air (fair)
ure (sure)	er (corner)		

HERE ARE SOME WORDS WHICH YOUR CHILD MAY FIND TRICKY.

Phase 3 Tricky Words			
he	you	she	they
we	all	me	are
be	my	was	her

TOP TIPS FOR HELPING YOUR CHILD TO READ:

- Allow children time to break down unfamiliar words into units of sound and then encourage children to string these sounds together to create the word.
- Encourage your child to point out any focus phonics when they are used.
- Read through the book more than once to grow confidence.
- Ask simple questions about the text to assess understanding.
- Encourage children to use illustrations as prompts.

PHASE 3 /j/ /v/

This book focuses on the phonemes /j/, /v/ and /w/ and is a yellow level 3 book band.

Dad Gets Fit
and
Jobs on a Jet

Written by
Georgie Tennant

Illustrated by
Rosie Groom

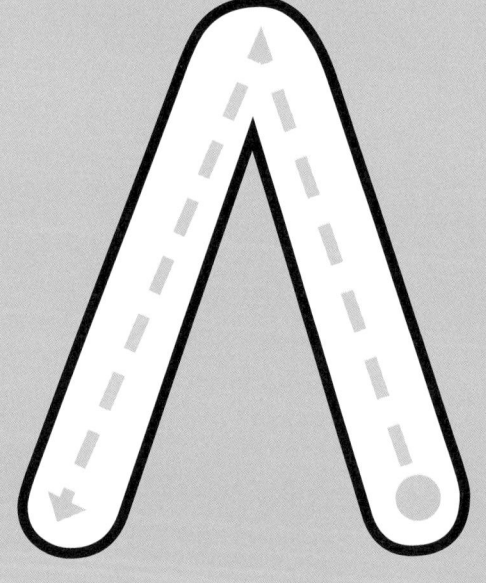

Can you say this sound and draw it with your finger?

Dad Gets Fit

Written by Georgie Tennant

Illustrated by Rosie Groom

Dad will get fit. He and Val will jog.

Dad is off! He huffs and puffs. He will win.

A dog runs up to Dad. It runs at his leg.

It is not fun! Val jogs on. Val will win.

Dad and Val jog. Dad huffs and Val puffs.

It is wet. Dad jogs in the mud.

Val picks Dad up. His leg is a mess.

Dad is off. He will win. He jogs on.

The jam van is in the gap.
Dad jogs in to Jack.

The jam is on Dad. Dad is a mess!

Val jogs up. Jack gets Dad in the jam van.

Dad will not jog to get fit. Val wins!

Can you say this sound and draw it with your finger?

Jobs on a Jet

Written by Georgie Tennant

Illustrated by Rosie Groom

Val visits Mum. Mum is the boss.

Jack gets the jet wet. It is a fun job.

Rav will get the bags. It is a big job.

Jess will get the tickets. It is a fun job.

Mum and Val get in the jet.

Jill tells the jet to go. It is a big job.

The jet is in a jam. It is in the fog.

Mum tells the jet to go. It will go up up up!

Vic gets Val a can to sip. But Val is sick.

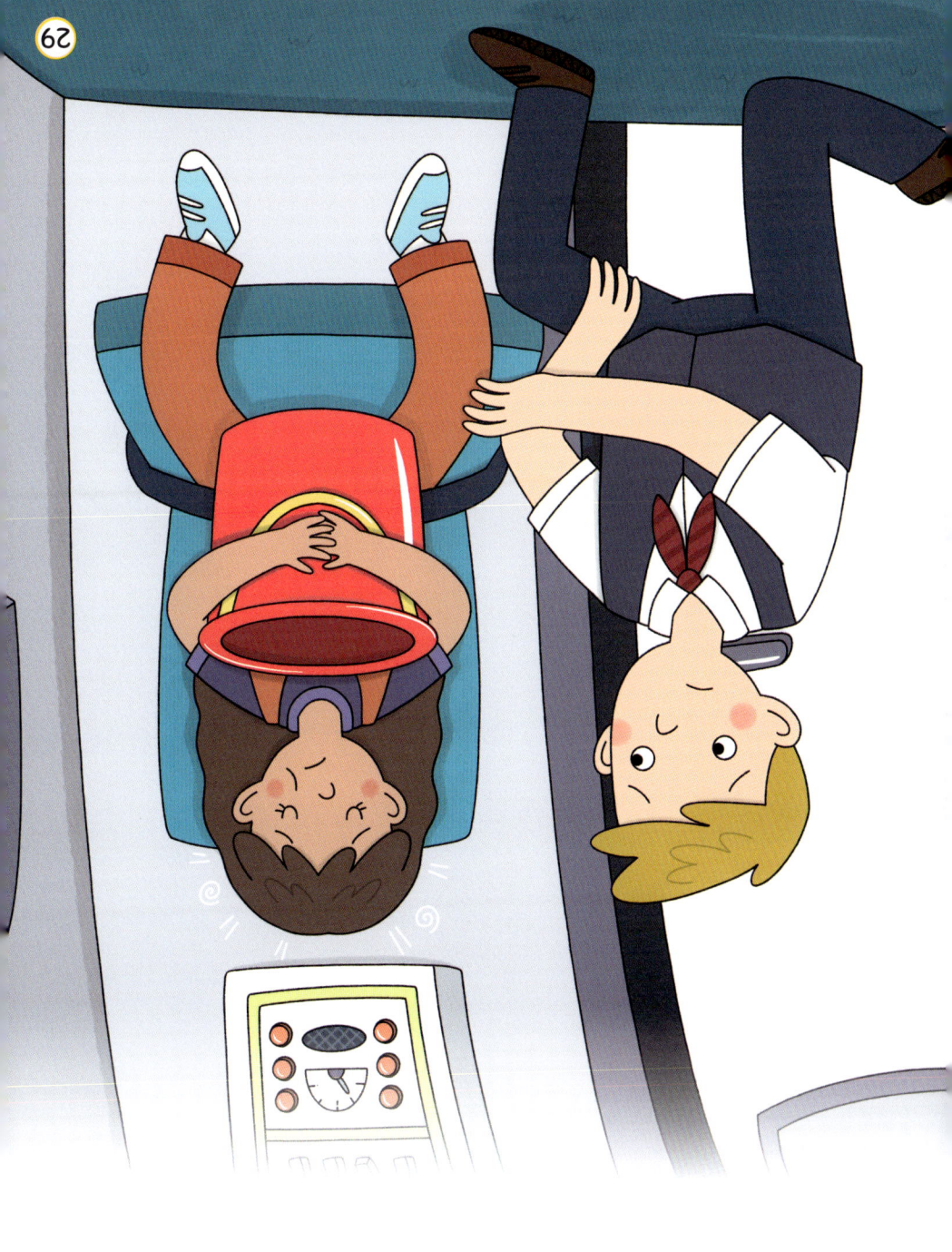

Vic gets Val a bucket. Not a fun job!

Val sits back. It is not dull on a jet.

Mum has fun at her job on the jet.

An Introduction to BookLife Readers...

Our Readers have been specifically created in line with the London Institute of Education's approach to book banding and are phonetically decodable and ordered to support each phase of Letters and Sounds.

Each book has been created to provide the best possible reading and learning experience. Our aim is to share our love of books with children, providing both emerging readers and prolific page-turners with beautiful books that are guaranteed to provoke interest and learning, regardless of ability.

BOOK BAND GRADED using the Institute of Education's approach to levelling.

PHONETICALLY DECODABLE supporting each phase of Letters and Sounds.

EXERCISES AND QUESTIONS to offer reinforcement and to ascertain comprehension.

BEAUTIFULLY ILLUSTRATED to inspire and provoke engagement, providing a variety of styles for the reader to enjoy whilst reading through the series.

AUTHOR INSIGHT: GEORGIE TENNANT

Georgie Tennant is a freelance writer who has written multiple stories for BookLife Publishing. She always knew she would be a writer as she used to present her school teachers with lengthy stories and poems for them to enjoy! Her two sons provide plenty of entertaining material for her writing, which usually appears on her blog or in the local newspaper as the 'Thought for the Week'. When she isn't writing she is working as a part-time secondary school English teacher, where she has the joy of inspiring slightly bigger children with the pleasure of reading good stories. She hopes to write good stories for them one day too.

PHASE 3

This book focuses on the phonemes /j/, /v/ and /w/ and is a yellow level 3 book band.

32

Dad Gets Fit & Jobs on a Jet
Written by Georgie Tennant
Illustrated by Rosie Groom

©2022 **BookLife Publishing Ltd.**
King's Lynn, Norfolk, PE30 4LS, UK

ISBN 978-1-80155-473-2
All rights reserved. Printed in Poland.
A catalogue record for this book is available from the British Library.